CONSTRUCTION ZONE

BY
TANA HOBAN

GREENWILLOW BOOKS, NEW YORK

the Publisher, Greenwillow Books, a division of William Morrow & Company, Inc., 1350 Avenue of the Americas, New York, NY 10019.

Manufactured in China by South China Printing Company Ltd.

First Edition
10 9 8 7

Library of Congress Cataloging-in-Publication Data

Hoban, Tana.
Construction zone / by Tana Hoban.
p.   cm.
Summary: Photographs illustrate the kinds of equipment and earthmovers found at construction sites.

ISBN 0-688-12284-1 (trade).
ISBN 0-688-12285-X (lib. bdg.)
1. Construction equipment—Juvenile literature.
2. Earthmoving machinery—Juvenile literature.
[1. Construction equipment.
2. Earthmoving machinery.]
I. Title.   TH900.H68
1997   624—dc20
96-5696   CIP   AC

FOR MIELA

RUBBER-TIRED BACKHOE

CONCRETE TRUCK

DUMP TRUCK

FORKLIFT CRANE

TAMPER

CHERRY PICKER

CRANE WITH CLAMSHELL BUCKET

CRAWLER BACKHOE

PAVER

ROLLER

FORKLIFT

GARBAGE TRUCK

IN THE CONSTRUCTION ZONE

RUBBER-TIRED BACKHOE
The rubber-tired backhoe digs holes and ditches. Its bucket scoops up the dirt and empties it into a dump truck to be carried away.

DUMP TRUCK
The dump truck hauls and dumps gravel and dirt. A hydraulic ram pushes the back of the truck up, the tailgate opens, and the truck empties its load.

BULLDOZER
The bulldozer moves on crawlers. Its blade pushes away the dirt and grass to prepare an area for construction.

FORKLIFT CRANE
This forklift crane lifts a bag of dry concrete mix, then releases the mix into the funnel of the on-site mixer. Water is added to the mix of sand, gravel, and cement to make concrete.

CONCRETE TRUCK
The concrete truck carries mixed concrete from the plant to the site. The container turns to keep the concrete mixed. Here, the concrete is filling cinder blocks to make a strong building foundation.

TAMPER
The tamper packs down a small area of dirt and gravel. The ground must be hard and flat to support construction.

PAVER

The paver carries hot asphalt in its hopper. As the paver moves, the sides of the hopper come together slowly, forcing out the asphalt. The roller flattens the asphalt to make the surface smooth.

CHERRY PICKER

The cherry picker lifts a worker. The person standing in the bucket can control the movement of the hydraulic arm.

ROLLER

The large roller presses dirt and gravel into a smooth, hard surface that can later be paved.

CRANE WITH CLAMSHELL BUCKET

A crane lowers a clamshell bucket onto gravel. The bucket's jaws open and take a bite of gravel. The crane lifts the bucket, then empties the gravel where it is needed.

FORKLIFT

The forklift picks up wooden pallets holding cinder blocks and tools and moves them around the construction site.

CRAWLER BACKHOE

The large crawler backhoe scoops up and moves gravel and dirt. It digs bigger and deeper holes than the rubber-tired backhoe.

GARBAGE TRUCK

The garbage truck has a hydraulic lift that raises and empties a trash bin into the hopper of the truck. The truck compacts the rubbish, then hauls it away.

TANA HOBAN's photographs have been exhibited at the Museum of Modern Art in New York City and in galleries around the world. Her more than fifty books for children are internationally known and loved, and include such classics as *Count and See*, *Just Look*, *Colors Everywhere*, and the innovative board books *Black on White* and *White on Black*. Born in Philadelphia, she now lives in Paris with her husband.

BOOKS BY TANA HOBAN

A, B, SEE!

ALL ABOUT WHERE

ANIMAL, VEGETABLE, OR MINERAL?

BIG ONES, LITTLE ONES

A CHILDREN'S ZOO

COLORS EVERYWHERE

DIG, DRILL, DUMP, FILL

DOTS, SPOTS, SPECKLES, AND STRIPES

EXACTLY THE OPPOSITE

I READ SIGNS

I READ SYMBOLS

I WALK AND READ

IS IT LARGER? IS IT SMALLER?

IS IT RED? IS IT YELLOW? IS IT BLUE?

IS IT ROUGH? IS IT SMOOTH? IS IT SHINY?

JUST LOOK

LITTLE ELEPHANT
By Miela Ford

LOOK! LOOK! LOOK!

LOOK UP, LOOK DOWN

THE MOON WAS THE BEST
By Charlotte Zolotow

OF COLORS AND THINGS

ONE LITTLE KITTEN

ROUND & ROUND & ROUND

SHADOWS AND REFLECTIONS

SHAPES, SHAPES, SHAPES

SPIRALS, CURVES, FANSHAPES & LINES

TAKE ANOTHER LOOK

26 LETTERS AND 99 CENTS

Board Books

1, 2, 3

PANDA, PANDA

RED, BLUE, YELLOW SHOE

WHAT IS IT?

WHITE ON BLACK

BLANCO EN NEGRO

BLACK ON WHITE

NEGRO EN BLANCO

WHAT IS THAT?

WHO ARE THEY?